# MARS
# AND
# THE INNER
# PLANETS

# MARS AND THE INNER PLANETS

## GREGORY VOGT

**FRANKLIN WATTS**
*NEW YORK/LONDON/TORONTO/SYDNEY/1982*
*A FIRST BOOK*

*FOR*
*PHYLLIS*

Cover photograph of Mars courtesy of NASA

Interior photographs courtesy of NASA

Diagrams by Vantage Art, Inc.

Library of Congress Cataloging in Publication Data

Vogt, Gregory.
Mars and the inner planets.

(A First book)
Bibliography: p.
Includes index.
Summary: Provides a brief history of planetary
studies and exploration, focusing on Mars and the
"inner" planets Mercury and Venus.
1. Planets—Juvenile literature.   2. Mars
(Planet)—Juvenile literature.   [1. Planets.
2. Mars (Planet) ]   I. Title.
QB602.V63      523.4      81-22029
ISBN 0-531-04384-3            AACR2

6

# CONTENTS

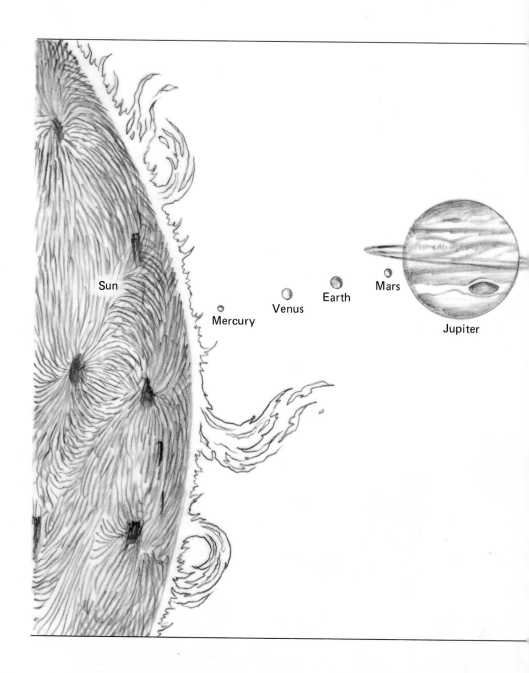

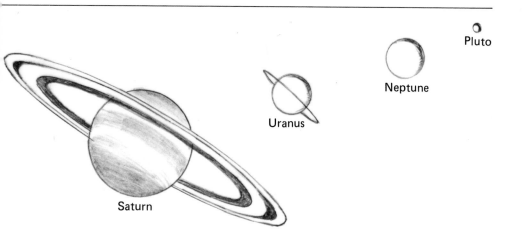

Saturn

Uranus

Neptune

Pluto

**Fig. 1.**
**Positions of the Planets**
**in Relation to the Sun**

# CHAPTER ONE

# THE PLANETARY EXPLORERS

## A SPACECRAFT LANDS ON MARS

In the orange glow of the Martian twilight, a strange white object passed slowly across the sky. For more than thirty days, the spacecraft had been overhead, gleaming brightly in the thin, crisp air. On this day, an important change would take place. The spacecraft would split in two, and one of the halves would descend to the surface of the planet.

In earth time, the date was July 20, 1976. It was exactly seven years to the day since the historic first walk on the moon. Eleven months earlier, a Titan III Centaur rocket had lifted off the launch pad at NASA's Kennedy Space Center in Cape Canaveral, Florida. Inside the top of the rocket were the *Viking I* orbiter and lander spacecraft. The spacecraft had been designed to study the surface and atmosphere of Mars, in part to determine if life existed there. Now, one of the most exciting episodes in space exploration was about to begin.

The *Viking I* lander was protected by a thin shell that would be ejected once it was no longer needed. There isn't much air surrounding Mars—only about 1/125 of that which surrounds the earth. Still, the sensitive spacecraft could be damaged from the heat generated by entry into the atmosphere.

At about 19,400 feet (5,800 m) above the area known as the Chryse Plain, the spacecraft's downward progress was slowed sufficiently by the air to allow a large parachute to be deployed. The parachute slowed *Viking* even further, providing time for the spacecraft to shed its protective shell. At 3,900 feet (1,200 m), the parachute was jettisoned, leaving the final phase of the descent to three clusters of rocket engines, each with eighteen nozzles. At precisely 4:52 A.M., Pacific Daylight Time, on that July 20, *Viking I's* three footpads gently touched down on the rock-strewn Martian plain. Twenty minutes later, a radio message from the spacecraft reached earth with word of the successful landing.

*Viking I* was not the first spacecraft to land on Mars, nor would it be the last. *Viking II,* which followed *Viking I* into space by one month, touched down considerably to the north of the first site on September 3, 1976. Both spacecraft were part of an ongoing investigation into Mars and the other planets in our solar system, in an attempt to learn, among other things, how each of the planets compares with our own planet, the earth.

## EARLY PLANETARY STUDIES

The study of the planets in our solar system actually dates back many thousands of years. At first, these studies consisted simply of observations. To the ancients, the clear night sky must have seemed filled with mysterious lights. Each night, these lights would appear to drift slowly westward across the sky, preserving their positions in relation to each other. It would be a long time before the cause of this procession, the rotation of the earth, would be discovered. Night after night, the patterns would be preserved, with new star groups appearing with the passage of the seasons. Except for an occasional comet or meteor streaking by, very little seemed to disturb the

Viking 1 *goes to work on the rocky Martian plain.*

heavens. There were, however, five lights that moved differently from the rest, but with a regularity all their own. To the casual observer, the motions of these special lights were not noticeable; they were too slow to be detected on any single night. It was only over a period of several weeks that the motions became easy to see. The rest of the lights provided a backdrop of reference points. These special objects wandered along some invisible highway in the sky, sometimes stopping, sometimes reversing direction, sometimes even growing brighter or dimmer.

To these five objects a special name was given—*planet*—a word that meant "wanderer." For a time, the sun and moon were thought to be planets also, so that the total number of objects then called planets was seven. The five fainter planets were given the individual names of Mercury, Venus, Mars, Jupiter, and Saturn.

Because the planets moved differently from the stars, they were given special attention by the early astronomers. Using primitive sighting tools these astronomers were able not only to map the planets against the backdrop of stars but also to actually predict planetary motions weeks or months in advance.

Except for refinements in the tools and techniques used to measure planetary positions, very little new information about the planets was gained until the sixteenth century. At that time, an important new idea began to emerge—the idea that the sun, and not the earth, was at the center of the universe. This new idea was not very welcomed because it reduced the earth to a mere planet, with only a single moon circling it. Many years would elapse before a sun-centered solar system would be generally accepted by everyone.

At the start of the seventeenth century, another important event took place. Around the year 1608, a new device was invented that would come to dominate astronomy in the years ahead. The instrument would reveal that each planet was not just a wandering light in the heavens but an entire world very different from our own. The new device was a telescope, and at first it was merely a curiosity. But only a year after it was invented, the great Italian scientist Galileo Galilei began building his own telescopes for scientific research. His instruments were far superior to those first invented. One night in 1610, Galileo pointed one of his telescopes toward the heavens and observed that the planets could be magnified into a disk shape while ordinary stars remained just bright pinpoints of light in the sky. He saw the phases of Venus and color variations on Mars. He discovered four moons circling Jupiter and the odd shape of Saturn (caused, though he didn't know it then, by the planet's rings).

Galileo's telescopes—he eventually built over a hundred of them, many for sale to noblemen—were primitive by today's standards. But with these devices objects could be magnified 32 times. His telescopes were a major leap forward in the field of astronomy. Later scientists would build upon Galileo's work and construct much larger telescopes, each providing more magnification than the last. With the newer telescopes, it became possible to make very precise measurements of planetary motions and to discover new planets in the sky. By 1930, with the discoveries of Uranus, Neptune, and Pluto, the list of planets was enlarged to nine.

Gradually, a picture of the solar system began to emerge. The planets nearest to the sun—Mercury, Venus, and Mars—were the most earthlike. None were bigger than the earth, and all were made of rock and possibly had oceans and atmospheres.

Planets much farther from the sun—Jupiter, Saturn, Uranus, and Neptune—were quite different from the earth. These planets were giants compared to the earth, and if they had surfaces, these were sunk beneath oceans of liquid gases. The remaining known planet, Pluto, was thought to be rocky in nature; but being so far from the sun, it was frozen solid and therefore quite unlike the earth.

## MODERN PLANETARY STUDIES

For about 350 years following the invention of the telescope, knowledge about the planets grew, but very slowly. Although telescopes 100 times larger than Galileo's had been built, they could only function from the surface of the earth, and the light-images reflected from the planets, before being magnified, had first to cross millions of miles of space and then penetrate the earth's atmosphere. The scientific data that could be gathered under these circumstances was very limited, and no firm conclusions could be drawn about the nature of each planet's environment.

Early on it was recognized that to verify the scientific data about the planets gained from telescopic observation, it would be necessary to actually visit them. To do this, the ancient propulsive device, the rocket, was combined with a wholly new vehicle, the spacecraft. The rocket could send modern scientific instruments via a spacecraft to the planet itself, where data could be gathered directly and transmitted back to earth by radio waves.

Dozens of spacecraft were launched toward the planets in the 1960s and 1970s, leading to a new understanding of the solar system. The planets were found to be far more exciting than anyone had ever dreamed.

## ROBOT EXPLORERS

The spacecraft used to explore the planets are remarkable collections of wires, gadgets, computers, radios, antennas, and more. Launched from the earth at speeds exceeding 25,000 miles (40,000 km) per hour, they are built to survive the high accelerations at liftoff. They cross millions of miles of space and function at a wide range of temperatures. They respond precisely to all radio commands. Inside protective enclosures are sophisticated instruments. For example, inside the *Viking* landers, which are simply six-sided boxes on legs, there was a trenching tool for soil sample collection, a miniature railroad system for transporting the samples, a weather station, a seismometer for Marsquake detection, a television studio, a radio transmitter and receiver, and a computer center. There were also two power stations, two chemical laboratories, three incubators, and three sets of rocket engines. All this was contained in a spacecraft smaller than a compact car.

Nearly every planetary spacecraft has some sort of camera system for taking pictures of the planets. The pictures sent back to earth are not actual photographs but images like the kind seen on television. The cameras scan the subjects upon which they are focused and break the images down into individual points that are measured for brightness. Then the measurements, in number form, are transmitted back to earth via radio waves. Computers on earth assemble the numbers in proper order and reconvert them to dots of light of varying intensity. When viewed on a television screen, all the dots merge to form the image.

The principal advantage of these pictures over those taken on earth using telescopes is the amount of detail that can be seen. The earth's atmosphere distorts our view of the heavens. Astronomers using telescopes on earth were lucky to be able to see features as small as a few hundred miles across on the planet Mars. On the surface of Mars, the *Viking* cameras could easily resolve small pebbles and sand.

Other scientific instruments carried aboard a spacecraft depend upon what scientists are hoping to learn. If the spacecraft will enter a planet's atmosphere, sampling devices will be used to sniff the gases, in order to determine what they are. Weather instruments will measure air temperatures, air pressures, and wind speeds. From orbit, an infrared spectrometer will scan for water, a chemical essential for life as we know it. A magnetometer will measure the extent of the planet's magnetic field.

If a planet is shrouded with a dense cloud cover, as Venus is, a radar wave emitter will be included. This device bounces

SUCCESSFUL PLANETARY MISSIONS LAUNCHED BY THE UNITED STATES
AND THE SOVIET UNION* TO MARS AND THE INNER PLANETS

| Name of Spacecraft | Destination | Date of Launch | Date of Encounter | Approach |
|---|---|---|---|---|
| Mariner 2 | Venus | 8/27/62 | 12/14/62 | Fly-by |
| Mariner 4 | Mars | 11/28/64 | 7/14/65 | Fly-by |
| Venera 4* | Venus | 6/12/67 | 10/18/67 | Impact |
| Mariner 5 | Venus | 6/14/67 | 10/19/67 | Fly-by |
| Venera 5* | Venus | 1/5/69 | 5/16/69 | Impact |
| Venera 6* | Venus | 1/10/69 | 5/17/69 | Soft-landed |
| Mariner 6 | Mars | 2/24/69 | 7/30/69 | Fly-by |
| Mariner 7 | Mars | 3/27/69 | 8/5/69 | Fly-by |
| Venera 7* | Venus | 8/17/70 | 12/15/70 | Soft-landed |
| Mars 3* | Mars | 5/28/71 | 12/2/71 | Orbit / Soft-landed |
| Mariner 9 | Mars | 5/30/71 | 11/13/71 | Orbit |
| Venera 8* | Venus | 3/27/72 | 7/22/72 | Soft-landed |

| Spacecraft | Target | Launch | Arrival | Mission |
|---|---|---|---|---|
| Mars 5* | Mars | 7/25/73 | 2/12/74 | Orbit / Soft-landed |
| Mariner 10 | Venus (V) Mercury (M) | 11/3/73 | V 2/5/74 / M 3/29/74 / M 9/21/74 / M 3/16/75 | Fly-by / Fly-by / Fly-by / Fly-by |
| Venera 9* | Venus | 6/8/75 | 10/22/75 | Soft-landed |
| Venera 10* | Venus | 6/14/75 | 10/25/75 | Soft-landed |
| Viking 1 | Mars | 8/20/75 | 6/19/76 / 7/20/76 | Orbit / Soft-landed |
| Viking 2 | Mars | 9/9/75 | 8/7/76 / 9/3/76 | Orbit / Soft-landed |
| Pioneer Venus 1 | Venus | 5/20/78 | 12/4/78 | Orbit |
| Pioneer Venus 2 (five probes) | Venus | 8/8/78 | 12/9/78 | Impact |
| Venera 11* | Venus | 9/9/78 | 12/25/78 | Soft-landed |
| Venera 12* | Venus | 10/21/78 | 12/21/78 | Soft-landed |

radar waves off unseen surfaces, and the wave patterns that form can tell us a great deal about the shape of the land below.

Some spacecraft may have special support equipment on board. The *Viking* landers, for example, had robot arms to scoop up samples of Martian soil for analysis in the landers' miniature laboratories. Motors are usually needed to point cameras and instruments in the right directions.

During a planetary encounter, the spacecraft is millions of miles from the earth. Radio commands, even though they travel at the speed of light, take many minutes or sometimes even hours to reach the spacecraft. The same is true for signals sent back to earth. Since so many different activities must take place during an encounter, direct control from earth would be impossible. Thus, the spacecraft is equipped with one or more computers to handle routine activities. Before leaving earth, these computers are fed a wide variety of programs relating to every function of the mission. The computers control the flight of the craft and take care of such "housekeeping" chores as temperature control. Instrument checks are done automatically. At any time during the mission, new programs can be fed into the computers to change the spacecraft's work assignments.

Maintaining communication with the spacecraft is vital to the success of the mission. Scientific data must be sent to earth, and new instructions must be sent to the spacecraft. To accomplish this, all spacecraft are equipped with at least two antennas. One is shaped like a dish and is usually able to tilt so that it can be aimed precisely at the earth. The dish-shaped antenna receives and concentrates incoming radio messages from the earth, and focuses and aims messages that are to be sent to the earth. The second antenna is rod-shaped and does not have to be pointed directly at the earth. This antenna may be several feet long.

Having more than one antenna on the spacecraft provides controllers on earth with flexibility in communicating with it.

Different radio frequencies and rates of transmission can be used. This helps to assure that, in spite of any equipment failure or radio interference, communications can get through.

Radio waves generally travel only in a straight line. To communicate, the earth and the spacecraft must be facing one another directly. But the earth rotates. This means that in order to maintain frequent contact with the spacecraft, there must be several widely spaced receiving and transmitting stations on earth. Thus, when one antenna is not in view of the spacecraft, another will be. Spacecraft launched by the United States have receiving stations in California, Spain, and Australia.

Keeping a spacecraft operating throughout a mission, which may last several years, requires a steady and reliable power supply. Depending on the destination, one of two power systems is used. For planets no farther from the sun than Mars, solar cells are usually chosen. Sunlight falling on the cells produces an electric current that powers the spacecraft. Some of the electricity used by the cells is stored in batteries for times when the sunlight is cut off, such as when the spacecraft passes behind a planet.

If a spacecraft is destined to go to Jupiter or beyond, solar cells cannot be used. At such great distances the sun's rays are not intense enough to power a craft. For example, by the time sunlight reaches Jupiter, it is only 1/25 as strong as it is on earth. So, for these missions, a different power source is needed.

Radioactive elements produce heat when they decay. This is the principle behind the Radioisotope Thermal Generator (RTG), in which heat produced by the decay of plutonium oxide is converted into electricity that powers the craft. Any excess heat produced is used to keep the spacecraft warm. In addition to using RTGs to power deep-space missions, RTGs were also included in the *Viking* landers on Mars. The Martian night lasts just over twelve hours. Solar cells do not function at night, and storage batteries would be drained of their power before dawn.

The last major component of a planetary spacecraft is its propulsion and attitude control system. The initial liftoff from earth is accomplished by a large booster rocket. Once the spacecraft is on its way, however, the booster is discarded. All further changes in speed and direction must be accomplished by onboard units.

Simple adjustments in the spacecraft's direction are made by small rockets placed in strategic locations on the spacecraft. A small thrust will start the spacecraft spinning. Then, when the craft is facing in the right direction, an opposing rocket will stop it.

Changes in speed, or velocity, are produced by a larger rocket, as are major changes in course direction. When a course change is needed, the spacecraft is first turned in the proper direction by its small rockets. The large rocket then fires for a carefully measured period of time, and the course change is made. To save fuel, changes are made as far in advance as possible. A small thrust made millions of miles in advance will accomplish the same as a large thrust will later, but the small thrust requires less fuel.

## FUTURE PLANETARY EXPLORERS

As exciting as they are, robot explorers have many limitations. Ultimately, the planets in our solar system will have to be visited by astronauts. This step may still be a long way off, however. The complexities of sustaining human life on roundtrip voyages to the planets are enormous. Yet, just as our curiosity has led us to walk on the surface of the moon, so our need to know about the planets may someday lead us to visit them as well.

# CHAPTER TWO

# MERCURY, THE PLANETARY OVEN

Swinging around the sun at a velocity of more than 107,000 miles (171,200 km) per hour, Mercury is the swiftest of all the planets. It is also the closest planet to the sun, and therefore experiences the strongest pull from the sun's enormous gravitational force.

With the exception of Pluto, which may be an escaped moon of the planet Neptune, Mercury has the most elliptical (egg-shaped) orbit. Its average distance from the sun is a mere 36 million miles (57.6 million km), about one third the distance from the earth to the sun and close enough to the sun to be continually scorched by its heat. Its *perihelion,* that is, its distance when it is closest to the sun, is 28.6 million miles (42.6 million km), while its greatest distance, its *aphelion,* is 43.4 million miles (69.4 million km).

Mercury's nearness to the sun makes it one of the most difficult of all the planets to spot. It never gets farther than 28° east or west of the sun. Planet-watchers have to begin looking for Mercury in the morning light, just before the sun rises, or at twilight, just after sunset. Mercury appears very low in the sky in either case. Due to the glare of the sun and the thick, hazy atmosphere surrounding the earth, Mercury is almost invisible

*This picture of Mercury, made up from 300 Mariner 10 photographs, shows the southern hemisphere of the planet. Note the thousands of craters that dot the surface, some of which show distinct raylike patterns.*

to sky-watchers today. Many modern-day astronomers have never seen it. Yet the discovery of Mercury dates back more than 2,500 years.

## EARLY STUDIES

Mercury may have been seen by prehistoric people, but the first record of its observation in the sky is from the year 265 B.C. Perhaps the early discovery of this planet can be attributed, at least in part, to the much cleaner skies in the days before the world became industrialized. At first, Mercury was mistakenly believed to be two planets. When it appeared in the morning, it was called *Apollo*.When it was seen in the evening, it was called *Hermes*. The Greeks later recognized that it was only one object, and the name Hermes was settled upon. In Greek mythology, Hermes was the messenger god and also the god of twilight who announced the rising of Zeus, king of the gods. Other peoples of the time named the planet *Woden*. One of the days of our week was named for the planet Woden—*Woden's day*, or *Wednesday*. The name *Mercury* is Roman. To the ancient Romans, who adopted almost all of the Greek gods but gave them different names, Mercury was the messenger god, the same as the Greek god Hermes.

Except for the time it took to orbit the sun, very little was known about Mercury until 1639. At that time the telescope, which had been invented just thirty years earlier, enabled astronomers to determine that Mercury exhibits phases, just like our moon. As we shall see later, Galileo had made a similar discovery about Venus some years earlier, and this knowledge helped prove that the sun really was at the center of our solar system.

With the construction of larger telescopes, our knowledge of Mercury increased. But even the largest telescopes were plagued by the thickness of the earth's atmosphere and glare from the sun. The bulk of our current knowledge comes from the development of a new technology. In the 1950s, radar waves from the earth were bounced off the planet. Returning

—23

wave patterns were analyzed for indication of surface shape and rotation. In 1974 and 1975, the *Mariner 10* spacecraft made three "fly-by" encounters and took pictures of half of Mercury's surface. The pictures were far better than those that had been taken from earth.

The radar studies of Mercury showed that the surface of the planet is very similar to the surface of our moon. The *Mariner 10* pictures confirmed this. The radar reflections also led astronomers to determine that Mercury's rotation rate is synchronized with its revolution around the sun. A Mercurian year is only 87.97 earth days long. But one rotation of Mercury is a full 58.646 earth days long. The rotation is exactly two thirds the length of its revolution. In other words, when Mercury has revolved around the sun twice, it has rotated on its axis just three times.

## A SUN THAT GOES BACKWARD

The rotation and revolution of Mercury and the shape of its orbit produce some strange effects. At times during the Mercurian year, the sun seems to stop in its motion across the sky, reverse course, go back, then reverse course again. At other places on the planet's surface during those same times, the sun sets, rises back up, then sets again in the same place. The apparent motion of the sun, as seen from any planet, is caused by a combination of the planet's rotation and revolution. As Mercury orbits the sun, its velocity changes greatly. Mercury moves much faster when it is nearer the sun than when it is farther away. At the farthest point, aphelion, the planet is rotating faster than it is revolving, and on the surface of Mercury it appears that the sun is traveling in one direction. At the closest point, perihelion, revolution is faster, and the sun seems to move the other way, giving the impression that it had actually changed direction!

Another surface effect caused by Mercury's motions relates to temperature. From the surface of Mercury, the sun looks 9 times bigger than it does from the earth. The tempera-

—24

ture is so high that if lead were present in the rocks on the surface it would melt out, forming silvery pools.

Some areas of Mercury receive much more heat than others. Imagine four houses built on the equator, each 90° apart. (See Fig. 2.) When Mercury is at its perihelion, House A is directly under the sun. A thermometer there would read about 764°F (407°C). Half a Mercurian year later, at aphelion, Mercury would have rotated only enough to have moved House B under the sun. Considering its greater distance from the sun, the temperature is lower for this house. Another half a Mercurian year later, Mercury is back at perihelion again, and House C is now under the sun. Once again, the temperature is high. When the planet is at aphelion a second time, House D has now rotated under the sun. Finally, after two full Mercurian years, House A is back under the sun, and once again the temperature soars. Every two Mercurian years, this process repeats itself exactly, causing Houses A and C to receive much more heat from the sun than Houses B and D. Scientists refer to the two spots on the surface where the imaginary Houses A and C would be located as *hot poles*. The areas where B and D would be located are referred to as *warm poles*.

Another dramatic feature related to temperatures on Mercury is their incredible range. At the hot poles, the temperature can reach 764°F (407°C), while on the opposite side the temperature can fall to −297°F (−183°C), a difference of almost 1,000°F (540°C). No other planet experiences such a wide temperature range.

## A PLANET OF EXTREMES
Although Mercury is one of the smallest of the planets, with a diameter of only 3,031 miles (4,850 km), it is also one of the most densely packed. Its density is over 5 times that of water. (The density of objects is usually given in comparison to the density of water.) Of all the planets, only the earth has a greater density. Scientists believe that this means that Mercury must have massive concentrations of metal in its interior.

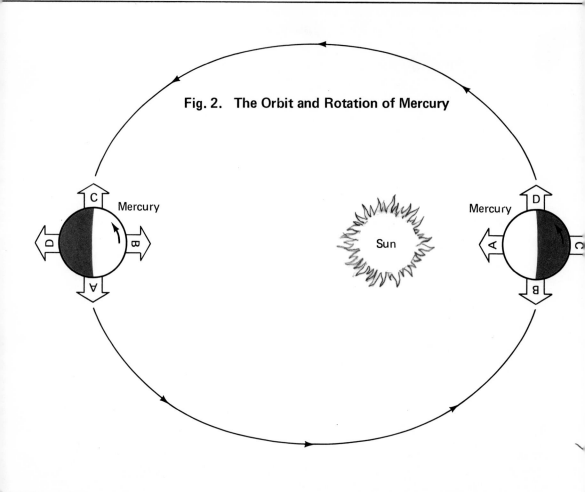

**Fig. 2. The Orbit and Rotation of Mercury**

*Mercury's elliptical orbit brings the planet close to the sun once during each revolution. Mercury's rotation is timed with the orbit so that at perihelion, House A or C is directly under the sun. At aphelion, House B or D is directly under the sun.*

When the *Mariner 10* spacecraft flew past Mercury in 1974 and then went into orbit around the sun, enabling it to fly past Mercury twice more the following year, the spacecraft radioed data back to earth that greatly surprised scientists. They discovered that Mercury has a magnetic field. Although this field is only 1 percent as strong as the earth's magnetic field, it should not have been there at all. The scientists had believed that for a planet to have a magnetic field, it must have both a fluid metal core and a rapid rotation rate. There was evidence for a metal core, as we have seen, but Mercury's rotation rate is extremely slow.

The discovery of Mercury's magnetic field and high density permits us to speculate on what the interior of the planet looks like. Like other rocky planets, the core of Mercury is probably made of iron and nickel, in a possibly partially molten state. However, unlike the other rocky planets, Mercury's core is thought to be exceptionally large—over 2,200 miles (3,520 km) in diameter. This is larger than our moon. On a percentage basis, Mercury has twice as much iron as any other planet in our solar system. Above the core is a layer of silicate rock called the mantle. (Silicate rocks are made up mostly of the elements silicon and oxygen.) At the planet's surface, the crust is also silicate rock.

The combined size and density of Mercury gives the planet an exceptionally strong gravitational field. Although nearly eighteen planets the size of Mercury would be needed to fill up a sphere the size of the earth, Mercury's gravitational pull is one third the strength of the earth's. A person who weighed 100 pounds (45 kg) on earth would weigh 38 pounds (17.1 kg) on the surface of Mercury.

Regardless of its relatively strong gravity considering its size, there is not enough gravitational attraction on Mercury to hold much of an atmosphere. The escape velocity from the planet—that is, the upward speed an object needs to exceed in order to leave the planet and not be pulled back—is only 14,010 feet (4,203 m) a second. Yet *Mariner 10* did detect signs of a thin atmosphere, composed chiefly of the gas helium. Still, the density of the atmosphere at the surface of Mercury is only about one trillionth of that on the surface of the earth.

From where does Mercury get its atmosphere? Scientists are not sure. The helium may come from the radioactive decay of uranium and thorium in the rocks. In such a case, the helium would be a by-product that would just leak out. Another possible explanation, and one that is more likely, is that the helium surrounding the planet comes from the sun. The fiery solar furnace continually expels matter into space. Helium could be caught, for a time, by Mercury's weak gravitational field. In either event, the atmosphere is only temporary, as the gas molecules seem to escape into space almost as soon as they arrive at the surface.

## THE SURFACE

Before the *Mariner 10* mission and radar astronomy studies, astronomers could only speculate on what the surface of Mercury was like. Some astronomers guessed that it might look like our moon. The radar studies and the *Mariner 10* photography both confirmed that guess to be correct.

Although *Mariner 10* only photographed half the surface of the planet, there is sufficient data to make a few general statements about the landforms there. The topography, or landscape, of Mercury can be divided into six main types of features. As with the moon, there are craters, basins, mountains, rays, and plains. There are also scarps, which are not usually found on the moon.

Craters on Mercury all seem to be of impact origin. More than 3 billion years ago, Mercury's surface was continually assaulted by the rocks and metal debris that whizzed around our solar system during its creation. As Mercury swung around the sun, its gravitational field swept up some of these fragments. Matter, from microscopic particles to asteroid-sized chunks of rock 40 miles (64 km) in diameter, crashed into the surface with explosive force. One especially large chunk exca-

*An artist's conception of the* Mariner 10 *spacecraft during its flyby encounter with the planet. Actual photographs of Mercury, sent back by* Mariner, *show the planet to be heavily cratered and possibly grayish-brown in color.*

*A close-up photograph of some of Mercury's craters. Note how several sharp, relatively new craters, such as the one in the center of the picture, overlap older, more smoothed-out craters.*

vated the 800-mile (1,280-km)-wide Caloris Basin. This basin is found on one of Mercury's hot poles. The word *caloris* means "heat" in Latin.

In the middle of Mercury's larger craters are central peaks that formed as a result of the impact. Other craters have fine dust particles that sprayed outward to form rays, or raylike patterns, that resemble the spokes on a wheel.

The largest of the craters on Mercury are called *basins*. The Caloris Basin, described earlier, is one of the largest known impact features on any of the planets or moons in our solar system. It is as large as the state of Texas. When the impact that formed the basin took place, waves in the surface rock shot outward. Some of these waves are still visible and are seen as rings of mountains circling the basin, giving the entire area a bull's-eye appearance. It is believed that some of the waves also traveled deep below the surface, causing a peculiar lumpy terrain to form on the exact opposite side of the planet. Similar effects occurred on the moon after particularly large impacts.

Between the rugged, cratered areas of the surface are relatively smooth plains called *planitia*. Following the most intense impact periods, there were quieter periods when lava welled up from the interior and the entire planet began to cool off and shrink in size. Surface cracks formed, allowing the molten material to move upward. Lava pools formed in the craters and hardened, turning the pockmarked surfaces into relatively smooth plains.

During the cooling periods, large sections of the surface also dropped downward into the surface cracks. This produced *scarps,* or cliffs, that can wander aimlessly for hundreds of miles across the surface. Sometimes, though, they will travel for great distances in neat parallel lines.

Little seems to have happened to the surface of Mercury after the cooling-off period. With no water and only the faintest trace of an atmosphere, the surface of the planet has hardly changed over billions of years.

# CHAPTER THREE

# VENUS,
# THE HOT HOUSE

## THE DEADLY BEAUTY

Like Mercury, Venus was once thought to be two planets, one appearing in the eastern sky a few hours before sunrise and the other turning up in the western sky shortly after sunset. The morning star was called *Lucifer,* which was Greek for "phosphorus," or "light-bearing" and also referred to Satan, or the devil. The evening star was called *Hesperus*, a name that meant "western" in ancient Greek. Eventually sky-watchers realized that the two were the same planet, and therefore a new name was needed. The name *Venus* was chosen. It was taken from the name for the Roman goddess of peace and beauty.

At first glance, Venus would seem to be a most appropriate name for the planet. Venus is the brightest of the planets in the nighttime sky. Only the sun and moon are brighter. Shrouded with dense, yellowish-white clouds, Venus glows brilliantly with reflected sunlight. More than once it has been mistaken for an unidentified flying object by an eager observer. If one knows where to look, Venus can even be seen occasionally during the day. Certainly, Venus is one of the most beautiful objects in the night sky. But down beneath the clouds is one of the most deadly and frightening planetary environments known. On the surface of the planet, the temperatures reach a searing 860°F (460°C). Atmospheric pressures are 90 times greater than on earth. The pressure on Venus's surface equals what it would feel like to dive below the ocean to a depth of 3,300 feet (990 m). Considering the surface conditions, Lucifer might have been the better name for this planet.

## THE SECOND PLANET

Since it is the second planet from the sun, Venus travels inside the orbit of the earth. This explains in part why Venus is such a brilliant object in the sky. At a distance of only 67.2 million miles (107.5 million km) from the sun, Venus receives approximately 2 times the amount of sunlight that the earth does. And because of the dense cloud cover, much of that light is reflected back into outer space.

Because it is closer to the sun than the earth is, the orbital period of Venus is shorter than the earth's. A Venusian year is not as long as an earth year. Traveling at a rate of 22 miles (35.2 km) per second, Venus takes 224.7 earth days to complete one orbit. Determining this was relatively easy. All it required were some precise measurements of the position of Venus in relation to the background of distant stars and some basic mathematics. However, determining the time it took for Venus to rotate was not at all easy. That kind of measurement requires being able to identify some sort of surface feature on the planet. As the planet rotates, the feature will disappear, then later reappear once the rotation is completed. Measuring the time it takes for the surface feature to reappear in the same place gives us the rotation rate for the planet. As we learned earlier, the surface of Venus is covered with dense clouds that hide all surface features.

In the early 1960s, the length of Venus's rotation was at last measured by bouncing radar waves off its surface. These waves were able to penetrate the cloud cover and reach the hard surface below. The rotation of Venus was discovered to be an amazing 243 days long! The length of its rotation is actually 18 earth days longer than its year! No other planet known has a rotational period longer than its year, that is, its period of revolution around the sun. One of the most interesting facts about Venus's rotation is that it is also backward in relation to its revolution. This backward spinning is called *retrograde rotation*. It makes the sun rise on Venus in the western sky and set in the eastern sky. This is just the opposite of what happens on earth. Figuring together both Venus's rotation and revolution, the length of a day on this planet is equal to 116.8 earth days. This is the longest day for any of the planets. On Venus, the sun rises and sets slightly less than two times during its year.

Because Venus is closer to the sun than the earth is, the planet is never seen in the southern part of the sky, as Mars, Jupiter, and the planets beyond Jupiter often are. Venus is observable only in the eastern or western skies. At its maximum distance from the sun, Venus forms an angle of 47°. This makes it possible to see Venus no earlier than three hours after sunset nor later than three hours before sunrise.

Another effect produced by Venus's nearness to the sun is that, like Mercury, it exhibits phases. Galileo was the first to observe these phases. While watching Venus over long periods of time, he noticed that when it approached its full phase, it appeared much smaller in size than when it approached its thin, crescent phase. This discovery excited Galileo because it was positive proof that at least one of the planets orbited the sun. If Venus circled the earth, Galileo said, its apparent size

*Venus as seen by the* Pioneer *spacecraft. The dark streaks in Venus's cloud cover show the sweeping motions of the planet's atmosphere.*

**Fig. 3. The Phases of Venus**

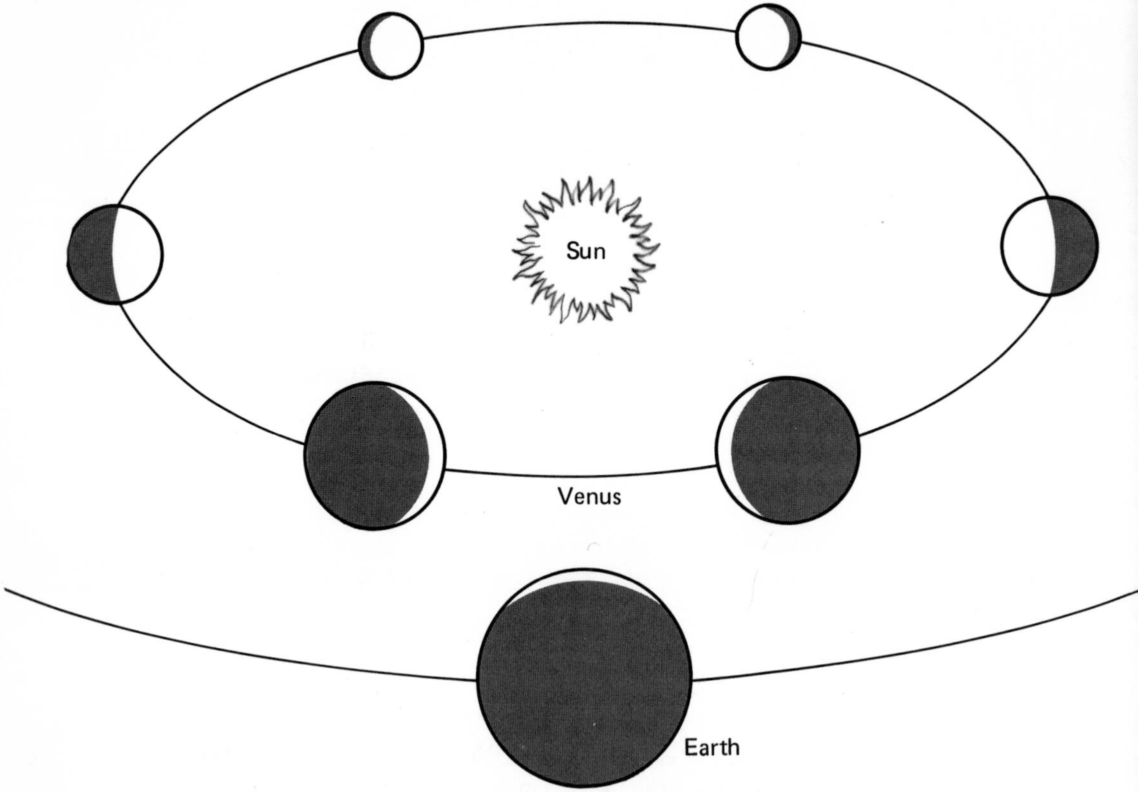

*As seen from the earth, Venus goes through phases and seems to change its diameter as it orbits the sun. Observing this, Galileo concluded that Venus must orbit the sun, not the earth. If Venus orbited the earth, its apparent size would not change.*

would not change. But it did change, and that meant that Venus passed behind the sun in its orbit. (See Fig. 3.)

Observing Venus, even by telescope, has not been easy. Besides the dense cloud cover, there is the problem that occurs when Venus is closest to the earth. At that time it is nearly in direct line with the sun and we can only see its dark side. When Venus is at its fullest phase, it is on the other side of the sun, more than 124 million miles (200 million km) farther away.

## ACID CLOUDS

Although Venus rotates very slowly, its atmosphere moves rapidly. On earth, masses of air tend to swirl around like pinwheels as they move from one place to another. On Venus, the upper atmosphere sweeps around the planet in one giant mass at speeds of up to 220 miles (350 km) per hour. A complete trip around Venus takes only four days. At the surface, however, the wind speeds drop drastically, to less than 2½ miles (4 km) per hour.

The cloudtops, as seen from a distance, appear brilliant white. This is due to reflected sunlight. Orbiting spacecraft, however, have shown the clouds to really be a yellowish-white. Space probes penetrating Venus's atmosphere have determined that the cloudtops are not made of water droplets, as they are on earth, but of droplets of sulfuric acid. The yellowish color comes from the sulfur, with perhaps some other element, such as iron, mixed in.

Descending to the surface of Venus would be a most hazardous journey for a human. Contact with the atmosphere would begin at 44 miles (70 km) above the planet's surface. Here we would encounter not only clouds made of sulfuric acid but also high-speed winds that would blow in one direction, and frigid temperatures of around −45°F (−43°C). As we dropped lower, the air would gradually begin to warm up. We would soon leave the sulfur clouds and enter a new cloud layer at 34 miles (55 km) down. This layer, we think, is made up of solid particles mixed with the sulfuric acid droplets from above, and it produces a rain that falls to the warmer regions below.

Still lower, just 30 miles (48 km) down, the temperature rises so dramatically that the particle and acid rain mix is broken down chemically into sulfur dioxide, oxygen, and water. The great heat drives the lighter materials back to higher levels, where they form into the original compounds again. On Venus, there seems to be an atmospheric cycle similar to the water cycle on earth, but with different chemicals.

The last cloud layer is broken through at 30 miles (48 km) down. Here we encounter a layer of haze filled with lightning flashes and the unending roar of thunder. There are perhaps as many as twenty-five lightning bolts a second, all zigzagging in different directions. These electrical discharges are the source of tremendous radio static. Now the temperature has risen to 194°F (90°C) and is still climbing rapidly as we continue our descent.

For the remaining 18½ miles (30 km) to the surface, the air has calmed considerably. Wind speeds have dropped to 60 miles (96 km) per hour and will continue to diminish until we reach the surface, where the air is almost completely still. In this last part of the atmosphere the air is almost entirely carbon dioxide with a small percentage of nitrogen. It is clean, but vision is obscured. The air pressure, which was very low up above, is beginning to rise more rapidly than the temperature. By the time the surface is reached, pressures are 90 times greater than at sea level on earth, and looking through the air on Venus is almost like looking through water. Distant objects seem to shimmer. Only the nearest objects appear in sharp detail. Overhead, the sun is only a reddish glow.

Moving along Venus's surface would be a slow, difficult process. The extreme density of the Venusian air would make it seem almost like walking through water. Surface winds would create a significant problem. Even slight winds would have great force in such high-density air.

## THE GREENHOUSE EFFECT

On the surface of Venus, the temperature is a blistering 860°F (460°C). On earth, temperatures vary with the day/night cycle and with latitude. On Venus, this is not so. From the day side to the night side, from the equator to the poles, the temperatures remain remarkably high. Even on the dark side the temperatures are so high that the rocks there glow a dull red, like the coils on an electric range.

The source of this great heat is, of course, the sun. The temperatures on Venus are higher than those on Mercury, even though Mercury is much closer to the sun. The important factors here are Venus's dense cloud cover and the carbon dioxide atmosphere, which together act as a heat trap. Sunlight that hits the planet's surface becomes heat. As the heat tries to escape back into space, the clouds and the atmosphere hold it in. This process is very similar to what happens inside of a closed car in the summer. Once trapped in the lower atmosphere of Venus, the heat spreads around the planet to the polar and dark-side regions. This heating of Venus's atmosphere has been called the *greenhouse effect* because it is the same way greenhouses stay warm.

## THE SURFACE REVEALED

For years astronomers wondered what the surface of Venus looked like. The cloud cover blocked any direct observation. Then, the radar techniques used to determine Venus's rotation rate were used with great success in surface mapping. Radar waves sent from earth and orbiting spacecraft pierced the clouds, enabling scientists to identify many land features.

Although the surface temperatures on Venus are far too

high for oceans of water to exist there, two huge continent-like features have been located. One of these "continents" is centered high in the northern hemisphere and is about as large as the United States. Mountains found in this area are as high as the earth's Mt. Everest. The other region is just south of the equator and is about half the size of Africa.

Most of the surface of Venus, about 60 percent, is relatively flat plain. Elevations vary by no more than about 3,300 feet (990 m). Venus has many craters, which range in diameter up to 370 miles (600 km), with depths from 660 to 2,300 feet (198 to 690 m). Many of these craters have central peaks, as do the craters of the moon and Mercury, and are, presumably, impact craters.

The plains of Venus, which cover much of the planet and surround the "continents," are used by Venus mappers to measure elevation the way sea level is used on earth. The remainder of the Venusian surface, about 16 percent, lies below the plains in basins. If water could exist on Venus, these would be the oceans. On earth, a far greater proportion of the total sur-

Above: *an artist's conception of what Venus would look like without its cloud cover. In this picture we can clearly see the two continent-like areas, protruding above a plain, found by radar mapping of the surface. The highest point on Venus, Maxwell Montes, is seen on the left. Below: one of the continent-like features, called Aphrodite, as it might look closer up.*

*An artist's conception of Venus's rift valley region.*

face, 78 percent, is covered by ocean. The deepest parts of Venus are the canyons that were formed from rifts or cracks in the surface. The largest canyon lies 1.8 miles (2.9 km) below the plain and is more than 4 times the length of the Grand Canyon on earth.

## EARTH'S TWIN

If a space traveler from somewhere out in the galaxy were to visit our solar system, that traveler would immediately be struck by the similarities between the second and third planets from the sun. Both Venus and the earth are nearly the same size. Venus's diameter is 7,521 miles (12,034 km), just 405 miles (652 km) smaller than the earth's. The two planets have almost the same mass and density, and both have atmospheres. Earth astronomers have known of these similarities for years and have themselves called the two planets "twins." Now, thanks to modern spacecraft, we know that there are some important differences.

In examining the two planets closely, an important question arises. Why is Venus so different from the earth? The answer, in part, rests with the carbon dioxide atmosphere that keeps in the sun's heat. The earth may have as much carbon dioxide as Venus does, but most of it is locked up in the various carbonate rocks, such as limestone, and the fossil fuels, such as coal and oil. The atmosphere simply never had enough free carbon dioxide long enough to produce the same greenhouse effect as on Venus.

The answer to the first question leads us to another. Is it possible that the burning of fossil fuels, to meet the energy needs of the people of earth, will release enough carbon dioxide into the atmosphere to bring about the greenhouse effect on earth? Some scientists say yes. And if the answer to this question is yes, then our present studies of Venus may give us a look into our own future.

# CHAPTER FOUR

# MARS,
# THE SEARCH
# FOR LIFE

## TWO POSSIBILITIES

One of the most intriguing and exciting questions of our age has been, "Are we alone in the universe?" Our own planet, we know, is teeming with life. Close to one million different species exist here. Besides finding life in the obvious places—places with ample sunlight, water, and nutrients—life is also abundant in the most unexpected places. Living things can be found on ocean bottoms, where there is almost no sunlight and incredible pressures, and in the hottest and driest deserts. Microorganisms have been discovered living in the pores of rocks in Antarctica, and some kinds of plant life exist around boiling hot springs. Certain kinds of bacteria have even been discovered living in the cooling water pipes of nuclear power reactors, where they receive many times the radiation sufficient to kill humans. The planet earth is literally covered with life.

Considering the capacity of life to adapt to extreme environmental conditions here on earth, it is reasonable to believe that life could have formed to suit other planets as well. Looking at just the inner part of our solar system, there are two good candidates for the possible existence of life. Before radio

*A computer-enhanced Martian sunset as seen from the Chryse Plain. The blue in the photograph is part of the Viking spacecraft.*

telescopes, which "listen" to the sounds of the universe, and the spacecraft expeditions to it, Venus was thought to be a likely place for life to have formed. Many astronomers even thought of the planet as earth's "twin," and some imagined it was covered with lush jungles and swamps filled with dinosaur-like creatures. However, following the American *Mariner* and Russian *Venera* missions to Venus, and the radio observations made in 1956 of its temperatures, nearly all speculation about life there came to an end. Venus was discovered to be far too hot (above 600°F, or 316°C) to permit the complex molecules necessary for life to exist.

Mars was an even better candidate for harboring life. Although Mars is farther from the sun than the earth is, it is still close enough to receive the warmth considered necessary for the development of life. Its distance from the sun averages 142 million miles (227 million km). Its diameter is 4,217 miles (6,747 km), which is just over half the diameter of the earth. However, its density is much less than that of the earth. Its smaller size and a density of just under 4 times that of water (earth is over 5 times as dense as water) give Mars a considerably lower surface gravity than the earth's. A person who could jump 3 feet (1 m) high on the earth could jump over 8½ feet (2.6 m) high on Mars.

Although Mars is smaller than the earth and farther from the sun, it does have two significant similarities to the earth. A rotation of Mars lasts 24 hours and 36 minutes. This is just forty minutes longer than a rotation of the earth. Furthermore, the axis of Mars is tilted to almost the same degree as that of the earth. This means that Mars goes through seasons just as the earth does, but the seasons are almost twice as long because Mars's period of revolution is 687 earth days.

Mars was the first planet in our solar system—other than the earth, of course—that was proven to have a solid surface. In the late 1700s, astronomers looking through telescopes were startled to notice that the surface of Mars changed with the seasons. Like the earth, Mars had polar caps that seemed to change size. In the summer, the equatorial region of Mars changed colors. Normally red, which led to its nickname of "the Red Planet," the Martian surface would become much darker in summer. At first, it was suggested that the darkness was from vegetation growing there in the summer months. Much later, the real cause was learned: in the summer, shifting Martian sands exposed the dark, underlying rock.

These observations of Mars, although exciting, were not conclusive in relation to whether or not life existed there. Mars's surface was soon discovered to have a thin atmosphere that sometimes stirred up dust storms and hid the surface. Even on clear Martian days, it was not always possible to observe Mars because of its distance from the earth. Only once every two years or so do the two planets pass close to each other in their orbits. And because Mars's orbit is not as round as the earth's, some of these close encounters are not as close as others. (See Fig. 4.)

## MARTIAN CANAL CONTROVERSY

In 1877 Mars and the earth passed by each other very closely, and another discovery was made about the surface of Mars. This discovery touched off a controversy that was to last for nearly a hundred years. Giovanni Virginio Schiaparelli, an Italian astronomer and the director of the Brera Observatory in Milan, Italy, observed Mars through his telescope and drew rough maps of its surface. Some of the features he saw were linear, and so he called them *canali*, an Italian word meaning "channels." Schiaparelli assumed that the features were waterways. He first mentioned these *canali* in a scientific report published a year later. As the years passed, Schiaparelli continued to sketch Mars, and his maps became increasingly detailed, with large networks of *canali*, sometimes running in pairs. Altogether, he identified 113 *canali*.

Perhaps because from a distance Mars looked so much

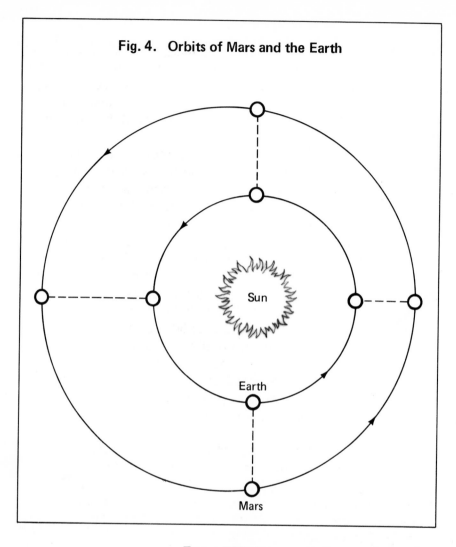

**Fig. 4. Orbits of Mars and the Earth**

Sun

Earth

Mars

*Every 780 days or so the earth catches up with Mars and makes a close pass in its orbit. Some close passes, however, are closer than others due to the two planets' different orbital shapes.*

like the earth, great public interest followed the announcement of the discovery of *canali* on Mars. The Italian word for channels was promptly mistranslated into the English word *canal,* a term that touched off widespread speculation over whether these "canals" might have been constructed by intelligent beings.

It was not until 1886 that other astronomers also began to see the "canals" of Mars. This was the first year that Mars was again in a highly favorable position for observation from earth. Astronomers in the United States, Great Britain, and France studied the Red Planet, and many saw the canals. An American astronomer, William H. Pickering, noted dark spots at the junctions of some of the canals and called them "lakes." Another American astronomer, Percival Lowell, built his own observatory (Lowell Observatory) in Flagstaff, Arizona, specifically to study Mars. Lowell counted 200 "lakes" but called them "oases" and ultimately identified over 500 canals.

It was Percival Lowell who really encouraged the belief in life on Mars. Lowell stated that the canals were not natural features but the work of "intelligent creatures, alike to us in spirit, though not in form." In three popular books on the subject, he pictured Mars as a dying planet whose civilization, in a desperate attempt to maintain life, used canals to transport water from the Martian polar regions to the more temperate zones.

Lowell's ideas were popular, and science fiction writers, most notably H.G. Wells (*War of the Worlds*), adopted the life-on-Mars theme. Even Schiaparelli, who had earlier considered the canals to be natural features, wrote in 1897, "The arrangements [of the canals] present an indescribable simplicity and symmetry which cannot be the work of chance."

Although many reputable astronomers could see the canals, others could not. Drawings of them by different astronomers showed many variations in canal patterns, lengths, and widths. Some astronomers argued that the canals probably did not exist at all, that they were just shadows on the Martian surface. Others thought the canals were fractures in the planet's crust, or ridges that rose above the surface. As late as 1964, one researcher suggested that the canals were really elongated sand dunes. By the early 1970s, no agreement had yet been reached concerning the canals or their true nature.

A major breakthrough came in 1972 when the *Mariner 9* spacecraft orbited Mars. *Mariner 9* took many low-altitude pictures of the planet. When these pictures were examined, no canals could be found.

What were the Martian canals? Probably shadows that relatively poor telescopic equipment plus overactive imaginations had made seem like surface features. With *Mariner 9*, the hopes for intelligent life on Mars were dashed. However, *Mariner 9* did not eliminate entirely the possibility of lower forms of life there, such as bacteria and microscopic plants or animals.

### THE MARTIAN SURFACE

While helping to solve the mystery of the Martian canals, the *Mariner 9* spacecraft was also enabling scientists to piece together the first nearly complete map of Mars. More than 7,000 photographs were taken and then joined together to form a huge mosaic of the planet. In this mosaic, Mars looks like two separate planets. A line drawn at roughly a 35° angle to the Martian equator divides two vastly different terrains. The southern portion consists of a heavily cratered landscape similar to the highlands of the earth's moon. Most of the craters, although well defined, show signs of erosion, indicating that they are very old. The craters come in many sizes; some of them overlap, some have central peaks, and many have flat bottoms. As with Mercury, Venus, and earth's moon, these craters were probably produced by meteorite impacts. There is one crater in the far south, the Hellas Basin, that is staggering in size. Believed to be the result of an impact with a giant meteorite, the basin could easily swallow up Alaska.

The northern portion of the map offered scientists more surprises. Relatively few impact craters were found here. Instead, this hemisphere had apparently been resurfaced by erosion and covered by lava flows and shifting dust and sand.

When *Mariner 9* first went into orbit around Mars, a dense dust storm shrouded the planet. Gradually, the storm began to abate. High points on the surface soon poked through the haze. The first of these points turned out to be the largest-known volcano in the solar system. Years earlier, scientists using telescopes had seen this feature and judged it to be a frost-rimmed crater. Seeing it close up for the first time, they were astounded at its size. At its base, it is just over 370 miles (592 km) wide. In height, it is 3 times the size of Mt. Everest. The lip of the crater is 50 miles (80 km) across. The distance from the top of the crater to its outer slopes is 15 miles (24 km), and the volcano ends in a series of sharp cliffs. The volcano was named *Olympus Mons*.

With further clearing of the dust storm, three other large volcanoes were discovered in what is now called the *Tharsis region*. Still another group of volcanoes is located in the *Elysium region*, some 310 miles (496 km) away.

Another surprise was the discovery of a giant canyon in the northern hemisphere of Mars. Scientists named this canyon for the *Mariner* spacecraft. They called it *Valles Marineris*. Stretching for some 2,500 miles (4,000 km), this canyon could span the United States. In places, it is four times as deep as the Grand Canyon and up to 124 miles (193 km) wide. The origin of the Valles Marineris was probably an ancient Marsquake that split the land open. The giant rift that resulted was later widened to its present state by wind and landslides.

One additional discovery, and perhaps the most important of all, was that of hundreds of braided, winding channels (not canals). The channels all had the appearance of having been carved out by running water. Although liquid water had not been found on the surface of Mars, there was substantial evi-

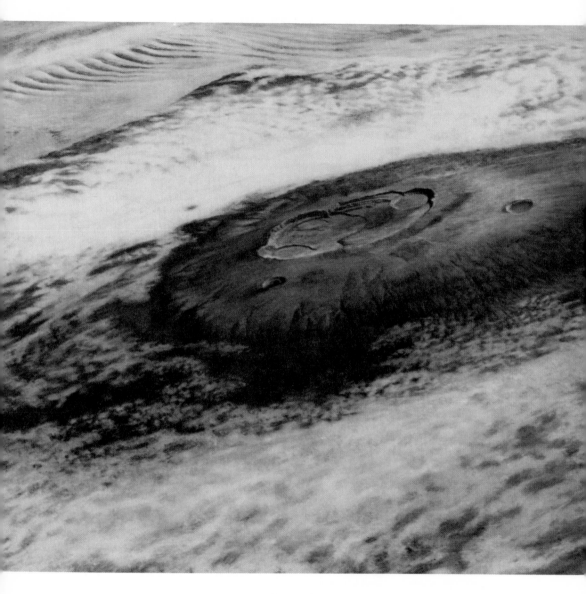

*An artist's drawing of Olympus Mons,*
*based on Viking photographs.*

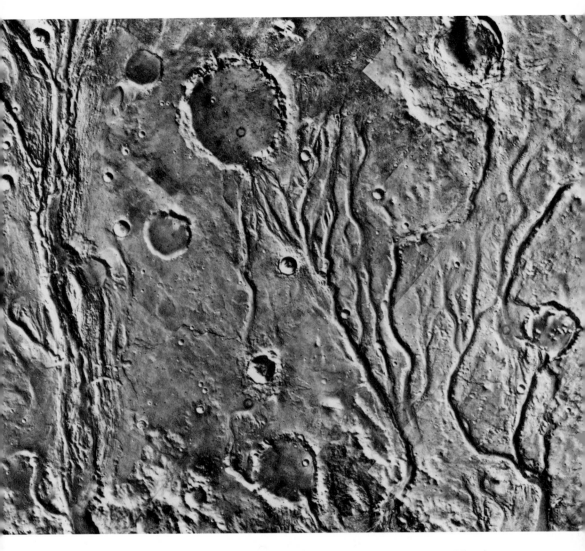

*Some of the channels found on the Martian surface, which may have been carved out by running water. At the end of some of the channels are meteorite craters.*

dence that it or some other fluid had once existed on the Martian surface in great quantities.

## FEAR AND PANIC

*Mariner 9* did not remain idle as it waited for the Martian atmosphere to clear. It occupied itself with looking at Mars's two moons. Almost 400 years ago, the astronomer Johannes Kepler said he thought that Mars would have two moons. Kepler reasoned that since the earth had one moon and Jupiter had four moons, Mars, which was in between the earth and Jupiter, should have two moons. Kepler's reasoning was silly and unsupported by any evidence. And Jupiter later turned out to have many more moons than just four. Nevertheless, Kepler was right. Mars does have two tiny moons circling it.

The Martian moons are named *Phobos*, meaning "fear," and *Deimos,* meaning "panic." They are both very small and potato-shaped. Phobos is roughly 17 miles (27 km) in length and 12 miles (19 km) in width. Deimos is about 9 by 7 miles (14 by 11 km). Pictures taken by *Mariner 9* showed both moons to be pockmarked with craters. The later *Viking* mission sent back even better pictures, and Phobos was shown to have odd striations, like the lines in sedimentary rock. These striations are probably fractures, resulting from a major impact with a meteorite.

Both Phobos and Deimos have unusual orbits around Mars. The two moons revolve in the same direction as Mars's rotation. Phobos revolves faster than Mars rotates, while Deimos revolves more slowly. The net effect is to make the two moons look like they are going in opposite directions. The difference in the revolutionary speed of the two moons is due to the difference in their distance from the planet. Close satellites must revolve faster than far satellites to stay in orbit. Phobos is only 3,100 miles (4,960 km) from Mars, while Deimos is 12,400 miles (19,840 km) away. Like the earth's moon, the moons of Mars always keep the same face turned toward the planet.

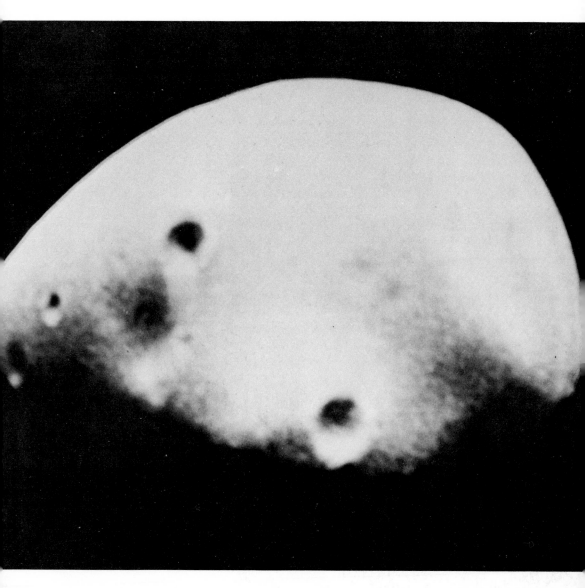

*Mars's two moons, Deimos (above)*
*and Phobos (over), as seen by* Viking.

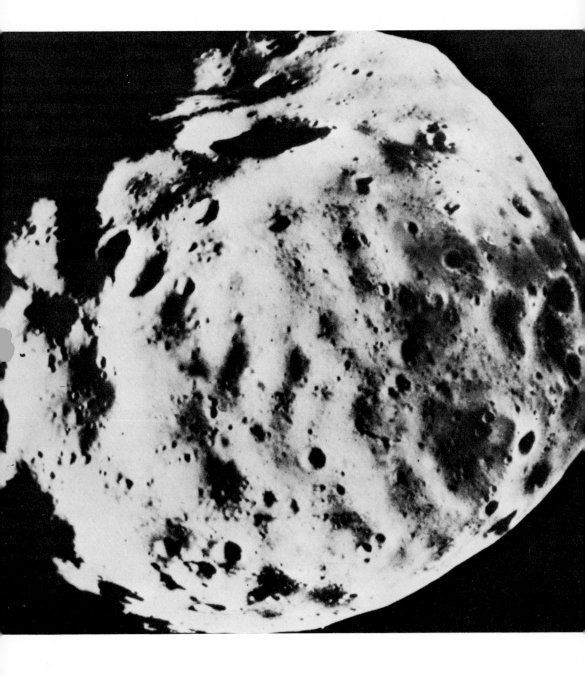

## THE VIKINGS

The first really good surface observations of Mars were made in 1976 by the two *Viking* landers. The *Viking* mission included two identical sets of orbiters and landers. This increased the chances that the mission would be successful. As it turned out, both spacecraft worked almost perfectly.

The two *Viking* landers came down in the northern portion of Mars. For convenience, Mars, like the earth, was divided into lines of longitude and latitude. *Viking 1* landed in the Chryse Planitia region at 22° north latitude. *Viking 2* landed considerably north of *Viking 1*, at 48° in the Utopia Planitia region. Both areas were believed to be smooth and sandy, and therefore safe for the landing of the spacecraft.

While descending to the surface, the *Vikings* made detailed analyses of the Martian atmosphere. As was suspected, most of the atmosphere was found to be carbon dioxide, although small amounts of nitrogen and water vapor were also discovered. At the surface, the Martian air pressure was found to be only 1/125 of the air pressure on the surface of the earth.

The first pictures taken by the landers astounded Mission Control on earth. Their "safe, smooth" landing sites were actually rock-strewn plains with boulders nearby as large as *Viking* itself! Any one of these boulders could have ended the mission. Had a lander tried to set down on one, it would have flipped over and been severely damaged.

As it turned out, however, the rocks at the two landing sites delighted geologists back on earth. Site 1 showed the greatest variety. Many of the rocks had flat, polished faces, the result of having been continually worn down by wind-blown sand.

The first pictures of the Martian surface were black and white, but later pictures were taken in color. The rocks were a rusty orange shade, which was later shown to be the result of iron oxide present in the dusty soil coating the rocks. The

orange dust was also determined to be the cause of the orang-ish-pink Martian atmosphere. Extremely fine dust particles suspended in the air give the atmosphere its unusual hue.

## MARTIAN WEATHER FORECAST

While the cameras on the landers were photographing the surface of Mars, other instruments on board were analyzing the weather. For a time, the *Viking* landers transmitted daily weather reports. Although severe temperature extremes were recorded, the weather on Mars was dull and repetitious. Daily reports were nearly identical: "Light winds coming from the east in the afternoon, changing to the southwest after midnight. Wind speeds gusting to 15 miles (24 km) per hour. High temperature in mid-afternoon, −22°F (−30°C). Low temperature, −122°F (−186°C), just after dawn. Barometric pressure, 7.7 millibars. Precipitation, zero."

There were only a few real changes in the Martian weather. One was a gradual drop in air pressure with the coming of winter in the southern hemisphere. Carbon dioxide was freezing out of the atmosphere, enlarging the polar cap. In another change, small amounts of water vapor would freeze on crater floors and along the flanks of volcanoes. With the morning sun, the ice would vaporize, forming a temporary fog.

## THE SEARCH FOR LIFE

The most important question the *Viking* landers hoped to answer was whether or not life existed on Mars. To probe for

Above: *the* Viking *spacecraft.*
Below: *a panorama of the* Viking I
*landing site, showing a rock-strewn*
*plain partially covered*
*by shallow sand dunes.*

signs of life, each lander carried a small scientific laboratory on board. Soil was scooped up by mechanical arms and sent along to the laboratories for analysis. The labs looked for microorganisms in the soil and carbon-based organic chemicals that are part of every living thing on earth. They also looked for the byproducts of photosynthesis, such as oxygen. Photosynthesis is the process plants use to make glucose (sugar) from water and carbon dioxide. Early test results indicated that photosynthesis did take place on Mars. Two other experiments tested for gases given off by animals when they eat and breathe. In one experiment, soil that had been placed in water gave off unexpectedly large amounts of oxygen.

The results of the search for life on Mars puzzled scientists. Some experiments indicated that life might be present, but no carbon-based organic chemicals could be found. After extensive analysis, scientists decided that no life had been detected on Mars.

In spite of the discouraging test results, the question of life on Mars is still open. The *Viking* landers sampled soil from only two different locations. And the experiments that were conducted, although sophisticated, were not exhaustive. The question of whether or not Mars has life may simply have to wait until the first human investigators arrive on the surface of "the Red Planet."

*An exact replica of the* Viking *landers and the equipment used to study Mars and test for life. The long tube in front is a soil scoop. The arm reaching up holds a weather station. And the dish antenna in the center was used for communication with the earth.*

# CHAPTER FIVE

## IN THE
## BEGINNING

One sun, nine planets, more than forty known moons, thousands of asteroids and comets, and billions of meteoroids make up the highly organized community we call the solar system. Thanks to the work of thousands of scientists and others from the past and present, today we know not only the positions of the planets and their moons and how they move in relation to each other but also some of the natural laws governing their motions. Gravity, magnetism, radiation, nuclear reactions, and many other forces in the universe are all at least partly understood today. With this body of knowledge, it has become possible for us to roughly piece together the story of how the solar system came into being.

According to some scientists, before the birth of the solar system our section of the universe must have been incredibly cold and dark. What was later to become our solar system was then only a formless, though not quite empty, void, a large bubblelike cloud of interstellar gas and dust. Imagine a cubic centimeter of air on the earth. The number of atoms found in that small bit of air would number 30 billion billion. In the interstellar cloud, the atoms numbered only 12 per cubic centimeter. A traveler passing through the cloud would hardly have been aware that it was there at all.

As thin as this cloud was, every object present in our solar system would emerge from it. The cloud contained the raw materials that would form the sun and the planets. Water, rocks, trees, and animals would all come from this cloud, too. But the cloud was far too thin for these objects to form on their own. Although the force of gravity contained in each atom and particle exerted an attraction over other atoms and particles nearby, the force was just too weak to bring them together. Something from outside had to start the collapse. Astronomers disagree on just what this something was. Some think that one of the spiral arms of the Milky Way, which is our own galaxy, moved through the cloud, causing a slight compression in it. This would have been enough to start the collapse. Other astronomers say that the collapse was probably started by the tremendous explosion of a nearby old star. The explosion, or *supernova,* would have converted much of the star's remaining matter to energy, and the shock waves that resulted would have compressed the cloud.

Regardless of the cause, the collapse began about 5 billion years ago. The immediate effect of the compression was to increase the density of atoms and dust particles. The closeness of the particles prevented outside starlight from entering, and the temperature began to drop. Even before the drop, the temperature was quite low, a frigid −370°F (−223°C), just 103°F (50°C) above absolute zero. (Absolute zero is the temperature at which all molecular motion is said to stop. It is the coldest anything can become.) As the temperature of the cloud dropped, so did any remaining resistance to gravity, and atoms and particles began to fall inward at an increased rate. Several globules of loosely knit matter formed. Each globule contained enough matter to make dozens of solar systems like our own. The globule that eventually formed our solar system continued to contract. Small whirlpools began to develop within the globules, causing the matter to break up into rotating fragments, one of which was to become our solar system.

The fragments of the original cloud continued their rotation as the matter fell inward. With the falling in, the speed of the rotation increased and flattened the cloud into a disk shape.

Not all of the matter in the cloud fragment that was to become our solar system fell inward. Some went into orbit around the heavy mass forming in the center. This mass, or sphere, was roughly 6.2 billion miles (9,900 million km) across, about twice the size of Neptune's orbit.

As gravity continued to pull matter inward, the center of the mass became much hotter than its outer edges. Soon it began to give off a dull glow from the heat of all the collisions of matter taking place in it. This was the *protosun*, or beginning sun. The protosun began spinning at a furious rate. It took on a liquid form, and a magnetic field developed, slowing the proto-sun down.

By now, 50 million years had passed since the compression of the cloud. The planets had not yet formed. They existed only as small globules of matter swinging around the protosun, sweeping up additional matter as they moved. They, too, took on a liquid state and began to glow.

The matter contained in each of the planetary masses depended upon its distance from the sun. The planets nearest the sun formed out of the heavier elements, elements that are usually associated with rock. Silicates, and various metals such as aluminum, magnesium, iron, and nickel, combined to form heavy, dense, rocky planets. The temperatures in the region of the inner planets stayed relatively hot. This made it impossible for the lighter elements, such as carbon, nitrogen, and hydrogen, and compounds, such as carbon dioxide and water, to change from a vapor state into liquids or solids. Most of this matter was driven from the center of the solar system to the region of the asteroids and giant planets.

At this stage, the planets had formed into what we call *protoplanets*. They began as asteroid-sized clumps but grew rapidly. With an increase in size, their gravitational fields grew stronger. This, in turn, attracted more matter and again increased their gravitational fields. In this manner, the protoplanets continued to grow, until they reached a size even larger than they are today.

For a time, the four inner protoplanets were solid-like, but the decay of radioactive elements within their interiors caused melting. The heaviest elements, notably iron and nickel, sank to the middle to form cores. Because it was nearest to the sun, Mercury contained the most iron and nickel. Its core extended nearly three quarters of the way to the surface. Venus, the earth, and Mars, each in turn, had a lower percentage of iron and nickel, and their cores were progressively smaller in proportion to their total size. (See Fig. 5.) With iron and nickel sinking to the middle, the upper layers of each planet became rich in silicate rocks.

During the formation stage, each of the four inner planets had atmospheres. Mercury, however, soon lost its atmosphere due to its nearness to the sun and a very low surface gravity. Mars, much farther away, was still able to retain only a very thin carbon dioxide atmosphere. It also had a very low surface gravity. Only Venus and the earth were able to hold onto real atmospheres.

The compression and collapse of the interstellar cloud, and the eventual formation of the protosun and protoplanets, took approximately 500 million years. Then, about 4½ billion years ago, the protosun grew so large and hot that its thermonuclear furnace ignited. Hydrogen began to fuse into helium and give off tremendous amounts of energy that were flung out into space. The protosun became a true star.

During the final stages of its birth process, the sun, like other young stars that astronomers are now observing, flung substantial quantities of matter outward. The rapidly moving matter, acting like a wind, swept clean any remaining hydrogen and helium from between the planets. When the solar mass was first formed, there was enough material to form two suns. Half of that material was returned to interstellar space by the solar wind.

From this point on, each of the four inner planets devel-

Fig. 5. Comparison of Planetary Cores and Diameters

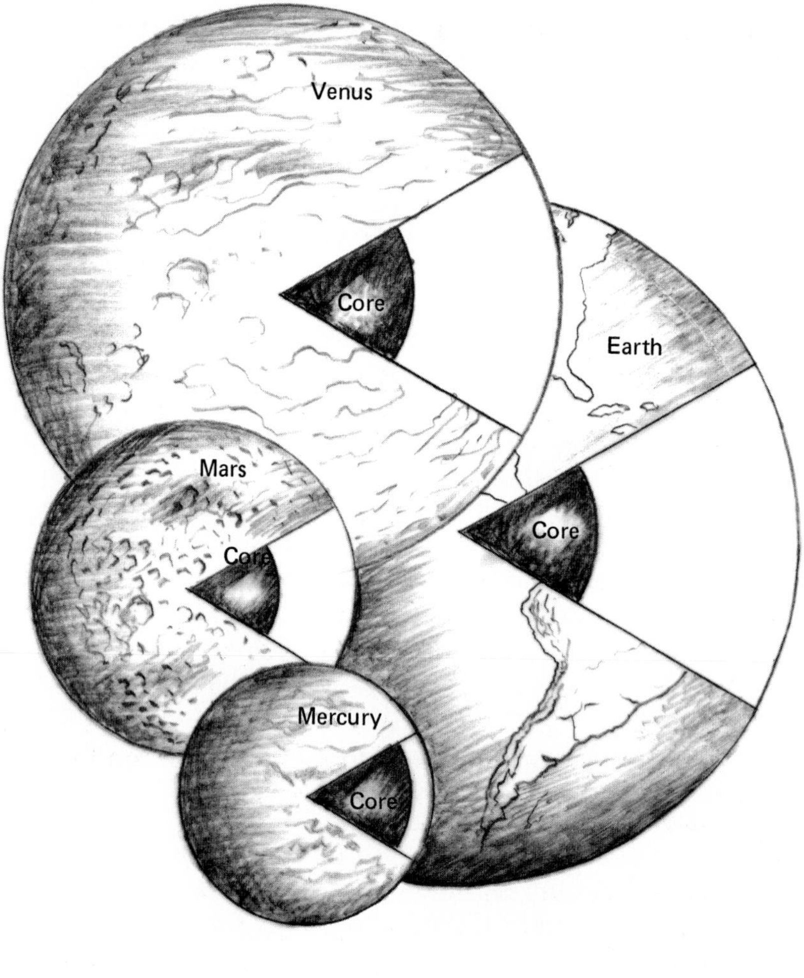

oped differently, to become what they are today. Mercury continued to be bombarded by leftover rocky debris. Its surface became cratered, like the highlands of earth's moon. Cooling of the interior caused the planet to shrink; this resulted in large cracks on the surface that settled and eventually formed into scarps. Lava welled up from the interior, filling in many of the craters. With no atmosphere to erode the surface, Mercury today looks almost the same as it did some 4 billion years ago.

The surface of Venus was also cratered by meteorite bombardment and covered, in part, by lava flows. But its surface was also affected by a very dense and hot atmosphere.

At first, the earth's surface was like Mercury's and Venus's, but its greater distance from the sun and different chemical composition permitted oceans to form. Then the continents were formed. They eventually split and drifted to their present positions. The earth's temperature was much more moderate than Venus's or Mercury's. All environmental conditions were perfect for life.

Mars, being farther still from the sun, also started with cratering and volcanic activity. Though no oceans developed, there is substantial evidence that water once flowed on its surface. Though no continents formed, one series of cracks produced a gigantic canyon. Volcanic activity continued, and the largest volcano in the solar system was formed on the surface. Water and wind erased many of the early surface features. Today, the winds are the main force of erosion on the planet.

The description of the events in the formation of our solar system, as just presented, is still theory, but theory based on a mass of scientific evidence.

With continued research, the development of new tools and more sophisticated spacecraft, and actual human voyages to other planets and even, someday, the stars, more answers may be found. But whatever happens, we can be sure that the universe will remain a place of wonders, just waiting to be explored.

# GLOSSARY

**Aphelion**—the farthest point a planet or other body reaches in its orbit around the sun.

**Atmosphere**—a layer of gases that surrounds a planet, moon, or sun that is held there by the object's gravitational field.

**Basin**—the largest craters on Mars.

**Canali**—an Italian word for "channels."

**Crater**—a hole or depression produced in the surface of a planet or moon by a meteorite hit or a volcanic eruption.

**Escape velocity**—the speed an object must exceed in order to break away from a planet, moon, or sun and not be drawn back by gravitational attraction.

**Gravity**—the force or attraction an object has that pulls other objects toward its center. Gravity is what keeps the planets in orbit around the sun and the moons in orbit around the planets.

**Greenhouse effect**—the gradual buildup of a planet's surface temperature by trapping the sun's heat with clouds and a dense atmosphere.

**Magnetic field**—the region around a planet that is filled with invisible lines of magnetic force coming from the planet's interior.

**Meteorite**—solid pieces of matter from space that sometimes crash into a planet's or moon's surface.

**Orbit**—the path that a planet takes around the sun or a satellite takes around a planet.

**Perihelion**—the nearest point a planet or other body reaches in its orbit around the sun.

**Phase**—the lighted portion of a planet or moon as seen from the earth or from any other celestial body.

**Planitia**—a plain on the surface of Mars.

**Protoplanet**—an early stage in the formation of a planet.

**Protosun**—an early stage in the formation of the sun.

**Ray**—a light-colored streak radiating outward from a crater.

**Retrograde**—a backward motion.

**RTG, or Radioisotope Thermal Generator**—a generator of electricity for spacecraft. RTGs rely on the conversion of heat produced by radioactive decay.

**Satellite**—a natural or artificial body that orbits a larger body in space.

**Scarp**—a long cliff on a planet or moon.

**Solar cell**—an electric power supply for a spacecraft or artificial satellite. Solar cells convert sunlight directly into electricity.

# FOR FURTHER READING

## BOOKS

Branley, Franklyn M. *The Nine Planets*. New York: T.Y. Crowell, 1978. (Good introduction.)

Gallant, Roy A. *National Geographic Picture Atlas of Our Universe*. Washington, D.C.: National Geographic Society, 1980. (Excellent source book.)

Kaufmann, William J., III. *Planets and Moons*. San Francisco: W.H. Freeman, 1979. (Somewhat advanced.)

O'Leary, Brian, and J. Kelly Beatty, eds. *The New Solar System*. Cambridge, Mass.: Sky Publishing Corp., 1981. (Beautifully illustrated, up-to-date, but rather advanced.)

## NASA MATERIALS (can be ordered)

*Atlas of Mercury*, NASA SP-423. Scientific and Technical Information Office, National Aeronautics and Space Administration: Washington, D.C., 1978. (Some technical material but primarily an atlas.)

*The Martian Landscape*, NASA SP-425. 1978. Same address as above. (Some technical material but well illustrated.)

*Viking Orbiter Views of Mars*, NASA, SP-441. 1980. Same address as above. Basically an atlas of *Viking* photography.)

*The Voyage of Mariner 10*, NASA SP-424. Scientific and Technical Information Office, Jet Propulsion Laboratory, California Institute of Technology: Pasadena, CA, 1978. (Technical material but well illustrated. Story of the *Mariner 10* spacecraft.)

# INDEX